This is my
dump truck

Written by Chris Oxlade
Photography by Andy Crawford

W
FRANKLIN WATTS
LONDON•SYDNEY

First published in 2006 by
Franklin Watts
338 Euston Road
London NW1 3BH

Franklin Watts Australia
Hachette Children's Books
Level 17/207 Kent Street
Sydney NSW 2000

Copyright © Franklin Watts 2006

Editor: Jennifer Schofield
Designer: Jemima Lumley
Photography: Andy Crawford
Dump truck driver: Peter Higton

Acknowledgements:
Christine Lalla/Watts Publishing p24; Lester Lefkowitz/Getty Images p25
The Publisher would like to thank Nigel Chell, Peter Higton
and all at JCB for their help in producing this book.

Every attempt has been made to clear copyright.
Should there be any inadvertent omission please
apply to the publisher for rectification.

A CIP catalogue record for this book
is available from the British Library.

ISBN–10: 0 7496 6538 6
ISBN–13: 978 0 7496 6538 8
Dewey Classification: 629'225

Printed in China

>Contents

My dump truck and me   6

Dump truck power   8

Wheels and tyres   10

The tipper body   12

Tipper rams   14

In my cab   16

Cab controls   18

Carrying soil   20

Tipping out   22

More dump trucks   24

Drive a dump truck   26

Dump truck parts   28

Word bank   29

Index   30

My dump truck and me

Hello! I am a dump truck driver.
This is the dump truck I drive.

▼ *My dump truck carries soil, sand, rubble and rocks on a building site.*

Dump truck power

All the parts of my dump truck are worked by the engine.

The engine is under the bonnet.

The engine is big and powerful.

The engine needs fuel to work. Fuel is kept in the fuel tank.

Fuel is poured in here.

Wheels and tyres

My dump truck has six big wheels. They let me drive over rough and muddy ground.

The wheels are nearly as tall as me!

The tyres have a chunky pattern. This makes them grip the mud.

The tipper body

I carry soil, sand, rubble and rocks in the tipper body.

The tipper body is made of tough steel.

There is a big hinge at the front of the tipper body.

▲ *The hinge lets the dump truck turn sharp corners.*

hinge

> Tipper rams

There is a powerful ram on each side of the tipper body.

This is one of the rams.

The rams tip up the body to empty it.

In my cab

I drive the dump truck from the cab.
The cab keeps me warm and dry.

cab

> *I have a comfortable seat to sit on.*

< **There are strong bars behind the cab. They stop rocks from hitting the window.**

Cab controls

I drive the dump truck with levers, pedals and switches.

There is a camera at the back of the truck.

This camera shows me what is behind the truck.

 Carrying soil

Today I am moving a heap of soil from place to place.

A digger loads the soil onto the tipper body.

Now I am carrying the load of soil across the muddy building site.

Tipping out

Now it is time to tip out all the soil.

I pull a lever to make the body tip up.

When the body is tipped right up, the soil slides out.

Now I drive forwards and lower the body again.

More dump trucks

Here are some more
dump trucks that I drive.

*I use this dump truck to
move rocks, sand and rubble
on a small building site.*

 *This giant dump truck could carry a whole house!*

Drive a dump truck

It takes a lot of practice
to be a dump truck driver.

*You have to learn how
to drive the truck safely
over bumpy ground.*

 You have to learn how to dump soil in the right place.

 You have to learn about all the dump truck's levers, pedals and switches.

Dump truck parts

cab

ram

mirror

tipper body

722

X04 XZ

JCB

light

bonnet

fuel tank

wheel

Word bank

building site – the place where a building is built

engine – the part of a dump truck that makes it move

fuel – the liquid that burns inside the drump truck's engine to make it work

hinge – the pieces of metal that join the cab to the tipper body so that the truck can bend in the middle

ram – a machine that pushes and pulls

rubble – pieces of stone

steel – a very strong metal

Websites

The dump truck used in this book is made by JCB. JCB make other kinds of construction vehicles, too, including diggers and loaders. You can log on to their special children's website at www.jcb.com/jcbjunior

29

Index

bars 17
bonnet 8, 28
building sites 7, 21, 24, 29

cab 16, 17, 28, 29
camera 19

engine 8, 9, 29

fuel 9, 29
fuel tank 9, 28

hinge 13, 29

levers 18, 22, 27
lights 28

mirrors 28

pedals 18, 27

rams 14, 15, 28, 29
rocks 7, 12, 17, 24
rubble 7, 12, 24, 29

seat 17
soil and sand 7, 12, 20, 22, 23, 24, 27
steel 12, 29
switches 18, 27

tipper body 12, 13, 14, 15, 20, 22, 23, 28, 29
tyres 11

wheels 10, 28
window 17